THIS Baptism Journal Belongs To:

_____

Baptism Date

_____

some ideas of what to write about in your baptism journal:

- -how my interview went with bishop
- -how i felt right before i was baptized
- -how i felt during the baptism
- -who baptized me?
- -was the water cold or warm?
- -who came to my baptism
- -what do i remember from the talks
- -how i felt when i received the holy ghost
- -the first time i repented after being baptized
- -how do i plan to stay clean and pure
- -draw a picture of you being baptized
- -how are you going to remember the covenants you made?

Made in the USA
San Bernardino, CA
27 April 2018